THE ESSENTIAL COLLECTION
HANDEL
GOLD

Published by
Chester Music Limited
14-15 Berners Street, London W1T 3LJ, UK.

Exclusive Distributors:
Music Sales Limited
Distribution Centre, Newmarket Road, Bury St Edmunds, Suffolk IP33 3YB, UK.
Music Sales Corporation
180 Madison Avenue, 24th Floor, New York NY 10016, USA.
Music Sales Pty Limited
Units 3-4, 17 Willfox Street, Condell Park, NSW 2200, Australia.

Order No. CH80179
ISBN 978-1-78038-751-2
This book © Copyright 2012 by Chester Music.

CD Project Manager: Ruth Power.
CD recorded and produced by Mutual Chord Studio, Guangzhou, China.

Previously published as Book Only Edition CH66792.

Book printed and CD manufactured in the EU.

CHESTER MUSIC
part of The Music Sales Group
London / New York / Paris / Sydney / Copenhagen / Berlin / Madrid / Hong Kong / Tokyo

I Will Magnify Thee
(from Belshazzar)

Composed by George Frideric Handel

Allegretto

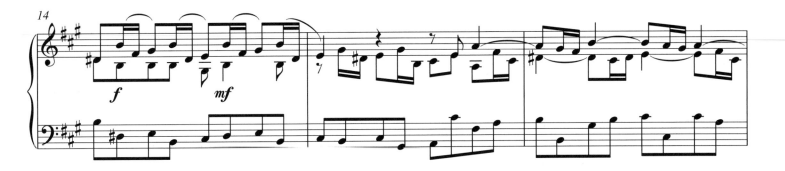

See, The Conqu'ring Hero Comes
(from Judas Maccabaeus)

Composed by George Frideric Handel

Alla marcia

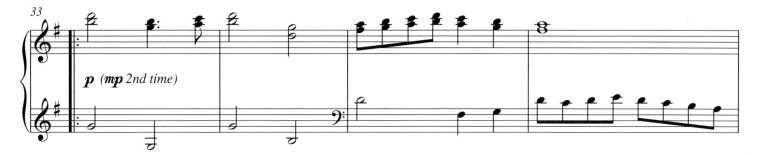

poco rall.

Zadok The Priest
(Coronation Anthem)

Composed by George Frideric Handel

Andante maestoso

pp   *crescendo poco a poco*

Con ped.

simile

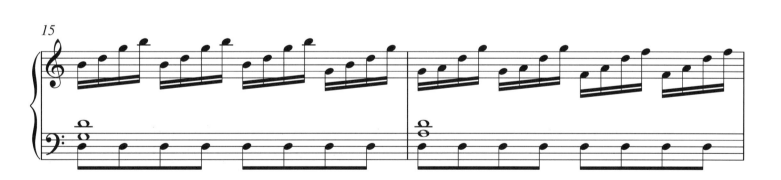

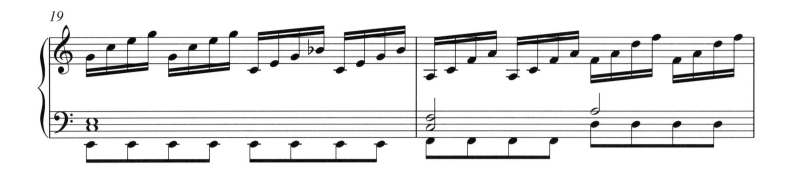

Ev'ry Valley Shall Be Exalted
(from Messiah)

Composed by George Frideric Handel

18

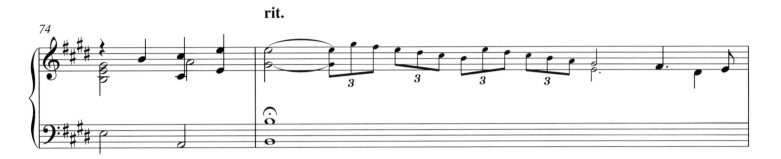

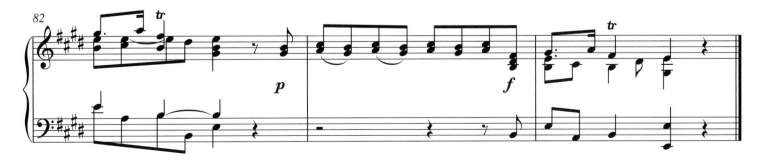

Hallelujah Chorus
(from Messiah)

Composed by George Frideric Handel

Allegro (♩ = 104)
sempre marcato

mf

I Know That My Redeemer Liveth

(from Messiah)

Composed by George Frideric Handel

Larghetto

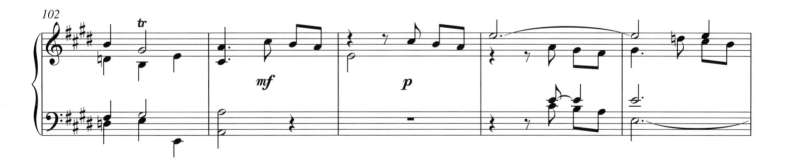

poco rit. a tempo

Let The Bright Seraphim
(from Samson)

Composed by George Frideric Handel

Andante

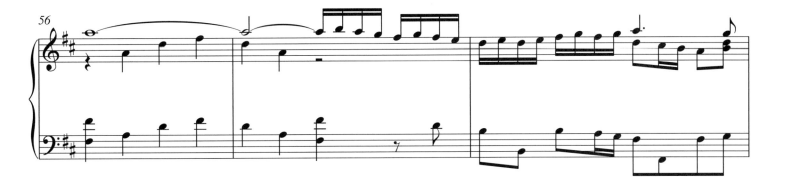

Dead March
(from Saul)

Composed by George Frideric Handel

The Arrival of the Queen of Sheba
(from Solomon)

Composed by George Frideric Handel

Allegro

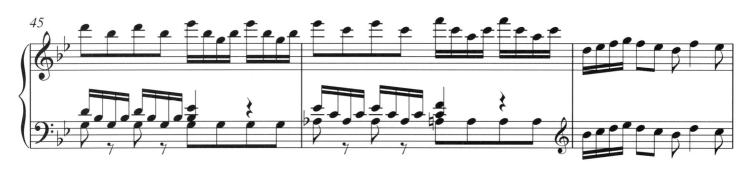

Lascia Ch'io Pianga
(from Rinaldo)

Composed by George Frideric Handel

Largo

Art Thou Troubled?

(from Rodelinda)

Composed by George Frideric Handel

Larghetto

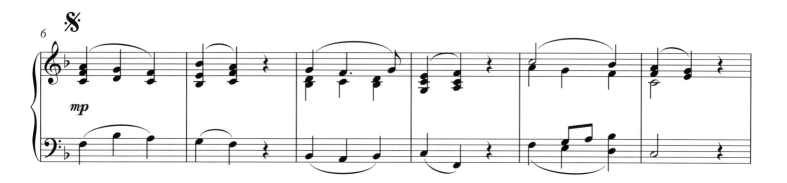

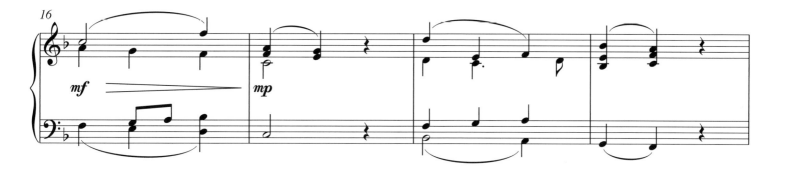

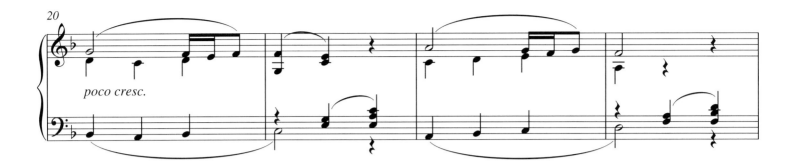

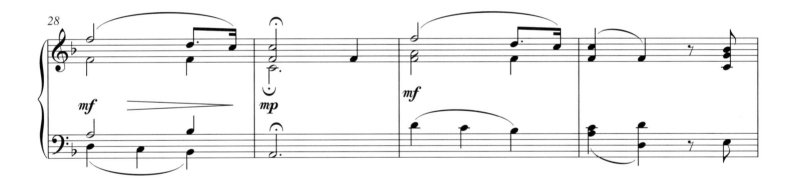

poco rit. a tempo   to ⊕ Coda

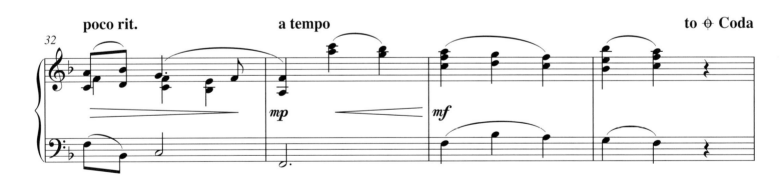

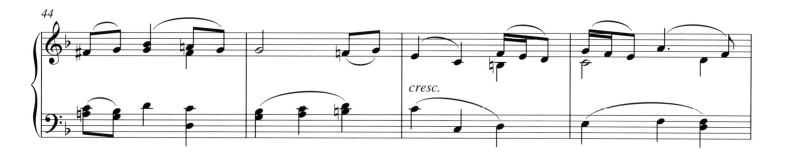

rall.   **D.S. al Coda**

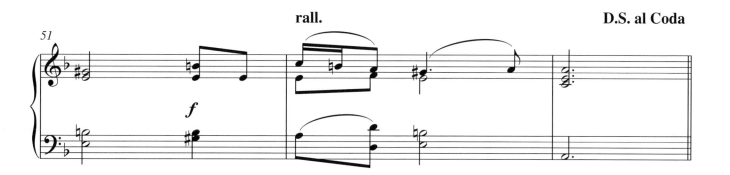

$\oplus$ **CODA**

Largo
(from Serse)

Composed by George Frideric Handel

Largo (♩ = 58)

p sostenuto

mf

rit.   a tempo

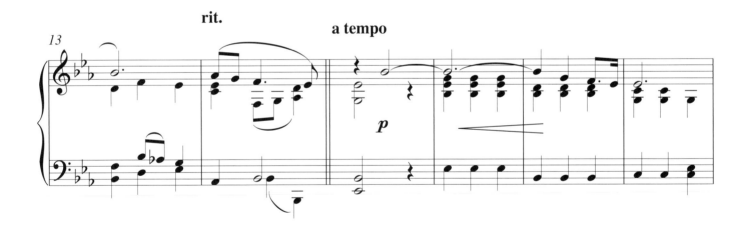

p

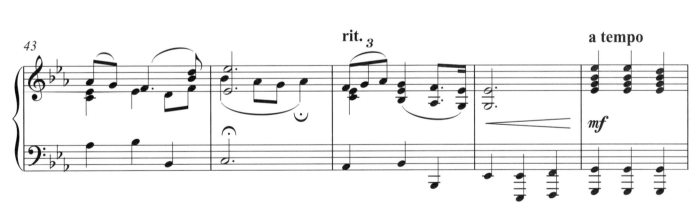

Aylesford Piece

Composed by George Frideric Handel

Vivace

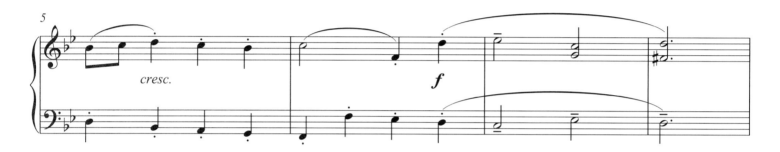

Invention in G major

Composed by George Frideric Handel

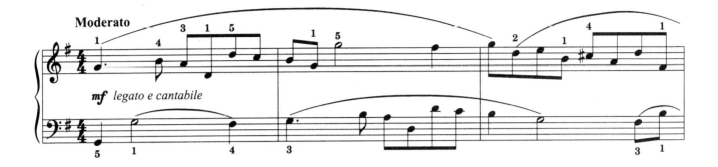

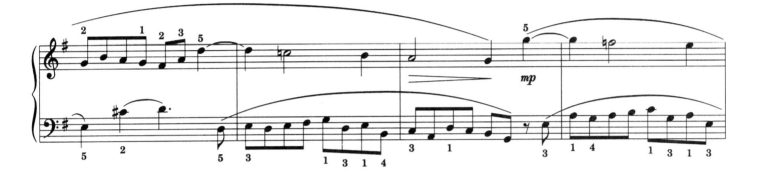

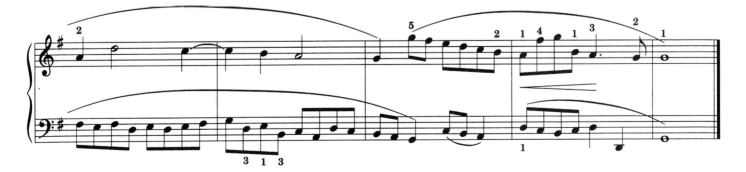

Boureé in G major

Composed by George Frideric Handel

Chaconne in G major
(Theme and Six Variations)
Composed by George Frideric Handel

Var. I

Var. II

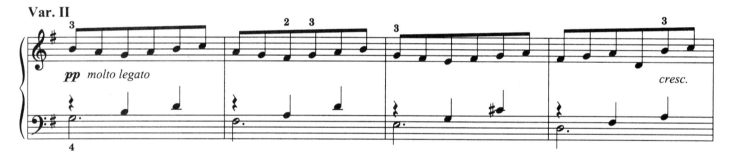

Var. III

Var. IV

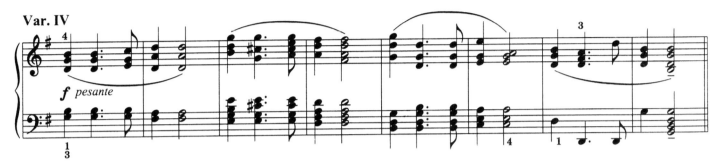

Var. V

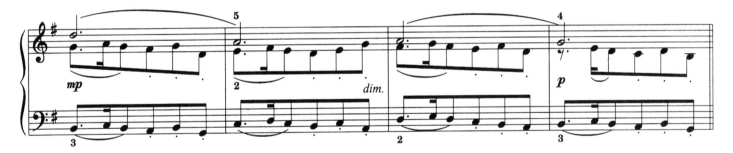

Var. VI

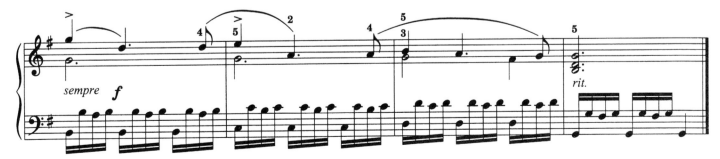

Fantasia in A major

Composed by George Frideric Handel

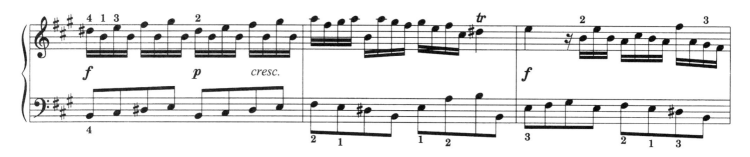

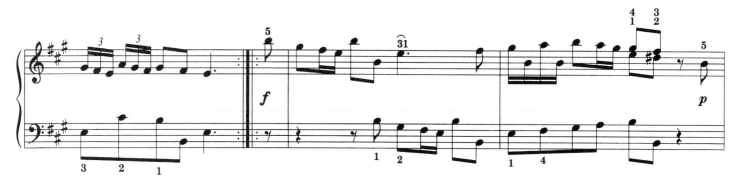

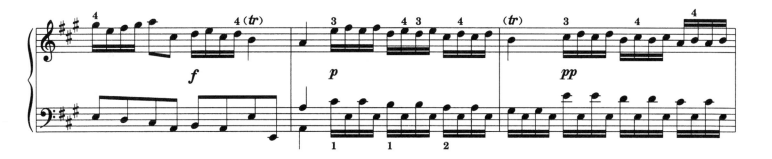

Gavotte in B♭ major

Composed by George Frideric Handel

Allegro con spirito

Risoluto

il basso ben marcato

allargando   **a tempo**

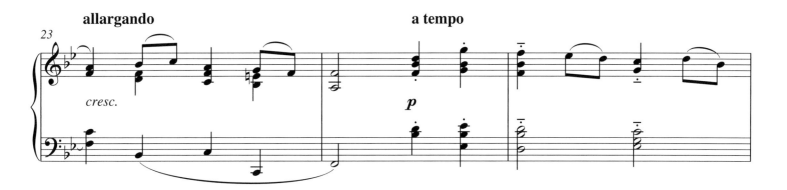

largamente

Giocoso

Intermezzo
L'istesso tempo

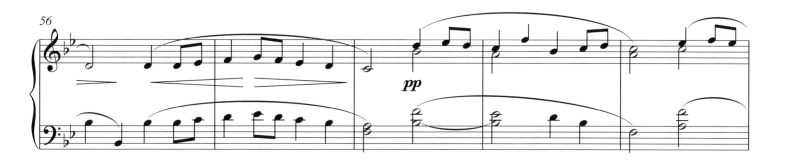

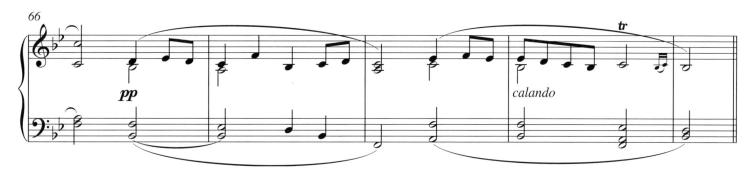

Gavotte

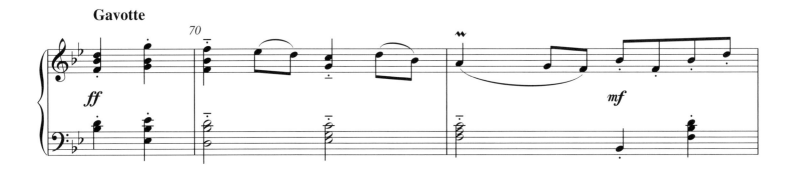

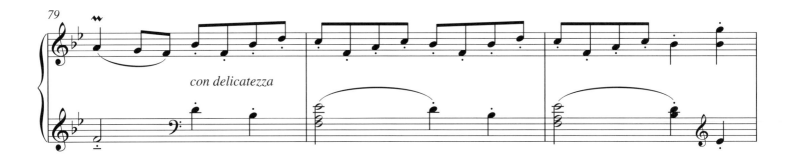

il basso ben marcato

Sarabande
(from Harpsichord Suite in D minor)

Composed by George Frideric Handel

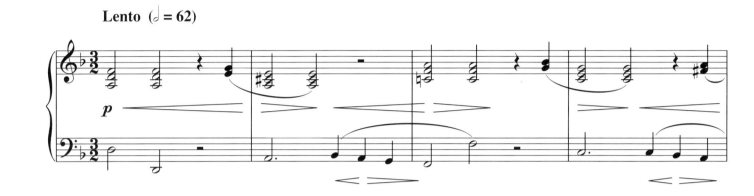

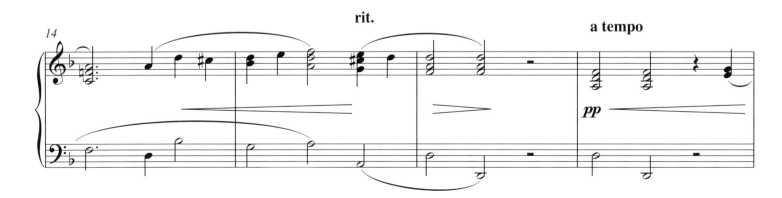

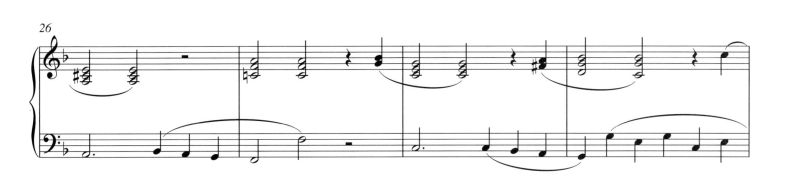

molto rit.

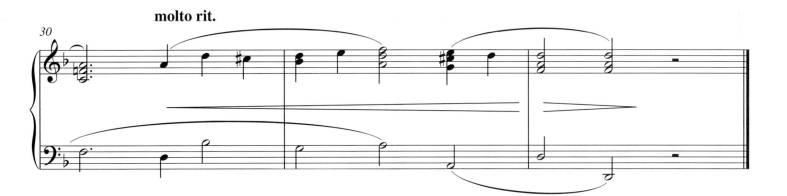

Suite No.7
(Allegro)

Composed by George Frideric Handel

Organ Concerto in F major
'The Cuckoo and the Nightingale'
(Allegro)

Composed by George Frideric Handel

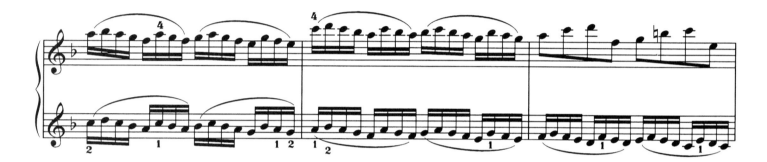

Harp Concerto in B♭ major
(Allegro moderato)

Composed by George Frideric Handel

Allegro moderato (♩=88)

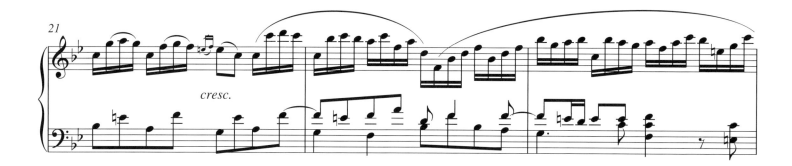

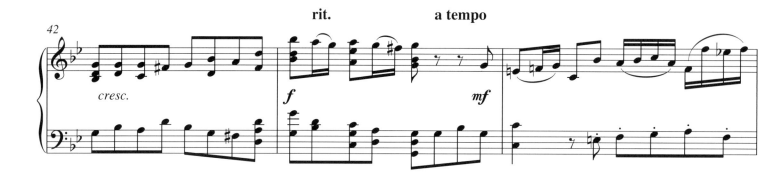

rit.   a tempo

The Harmonious Blacksmith
(Air and Variations)

Composed by George Frideric Handel

Moderato

Var. 1

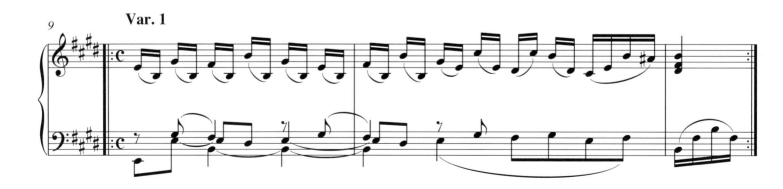

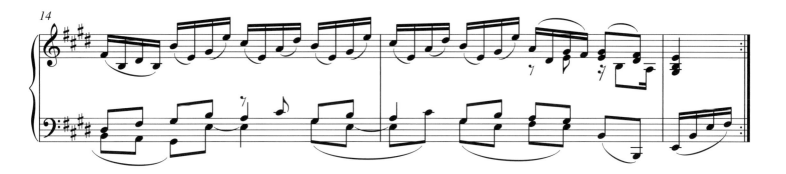

Var. 2

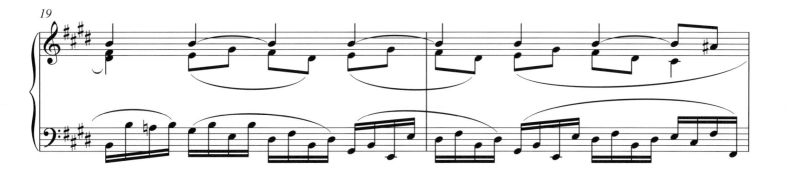

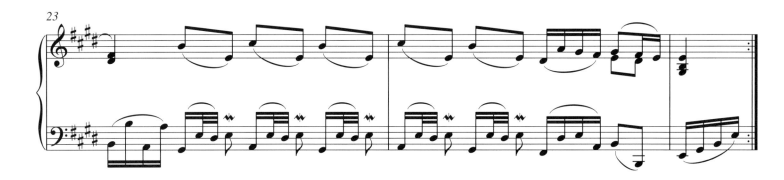

Var. 3

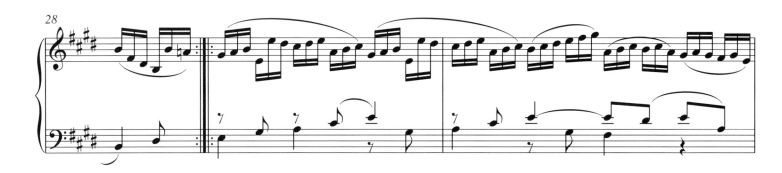

Var. 4

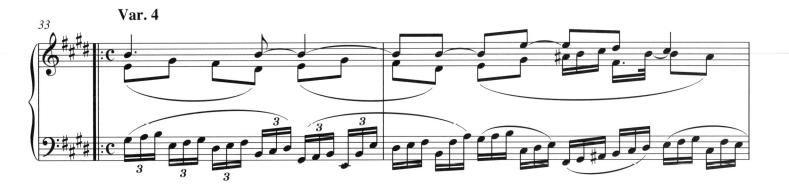

Var. 5

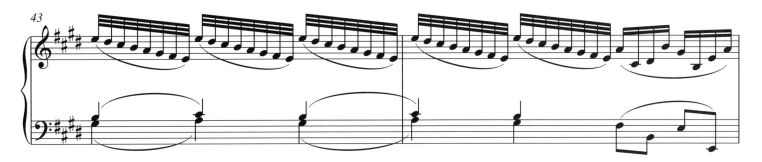

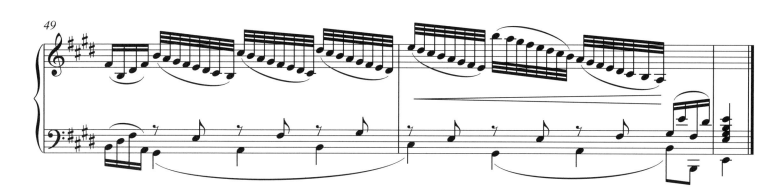

Air
(from Water Music)

Composed by George Frideric Handel

Allegro
(from Water Music)

Composed by George Frideric Handel

Allegro (♩ = 132)

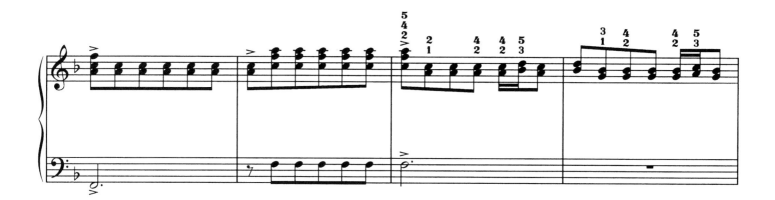

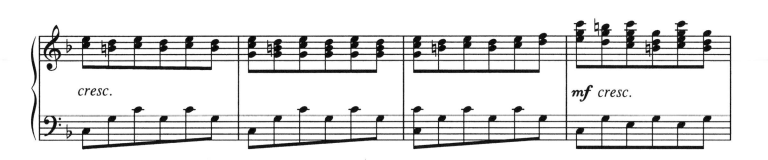

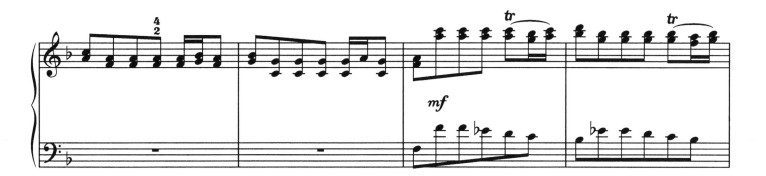

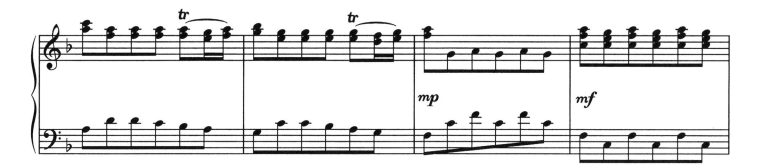

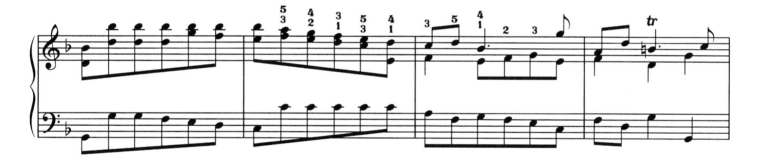

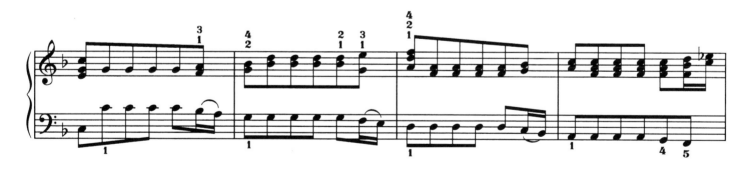

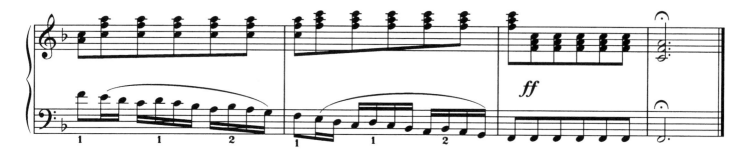

Hornpipe
(from Water Music)

Composed by George Frideric Handel

Alla hornpipe

Fine

D.C. al Fine

Siciliana
(from Music for the Royal Fireworks)

Composed by George Frideric Handel

123456789